HOW TO SAVE THE WORLD

How to Save the World

the World

In 12 Easy Steps

B Shawn Clark

How to Save the World – In 12 Easy Steps is a work based on an idiosyncratic form of verfabula (literary nonfiction) intended to make technical information more digestible to a broader audience. Resemblances in this work to real-life people or historical events should not be regarded as factual. Opinions expressed in this book are those of the author as expressed by the characters he has created, and should not be confused with those of anyone else.

ISBN: 979-8-9879174-2-8 (this paperback)
       979-8-9879174-1-1 (eBook)

Cover art by SRB McKenzie.
Book design by Aggregate Books.
First "printing" edition 2023. This addition: 2025

AGGREGATE BOOKS
ENGLEWOOD, FLORIDA USA
(AN IMPRINT OF A # OF THINGS, LLC)

WHOLE≳∑PARTS

www.12easysteps.info

FOREWARD

Not that long ago there was this crazy way in which the world, including almost all of the creatures that live here, were kept from being annihilated. MAD is what they called it. This madness (which stands for Mutually Assured Destruction) kept the peace between the United States and the Soviet Union. The two empires, so the theory went, held loaded pistols to each other's heads in the form of intercontinental ballistic missiles (ICBMs) weaponized to unleash a nuclear holocaust should either empire attempt to pull the trigger, or even flinch or bat an eye, that they had or were about to launch an attack.

Because the resulting holocaust would destroy both empires, the two sides decided that the better part of valor meant simply holding the gun steady to the temple of the other guy and not flinching a whole lot.

Or so the theory goes.

Sounds crazy, doesn't it?

Then something unnerving happened. The idea was floated by the United States that it could survive a nuclear war if they struck first.

FOREWARD

This idea was thought to sound a little less crazy if space could be weaponized to the point that missiles or maybe even laser beams from the sky could shoot down some of the missiles that would be launched by the Soviets in retaliation for a preemptive first strike launched by the Americans. "Star Wars" they called it. This seems like a long, long time ago in a galaxy far, far away. In fact, fittingly enough, it was right around the time when that Star Wars movie *The Empire Strikes Back* came out.

But why bring all that stuff up now?

The reason is that during the 1980s in America (and one would expect the rest of the world) suddenly the human species became acutely aware of the potential for its imminent extinction at the press of a button.

The probability that the button might be pressed in the very near future became more likely than ever. During this time, with the idea of purposeful mass suicide to save the world from being dominated by one empire over the other, your humble narrator was, well, a humble law student taking a class where he felt obliged to write his thesis on how and why the world should not do that.

His professor, Winston Nagan, emphasized the importance of having international laws that are not so much law unto themselves but, rather, create a framework upon which the peoples of the world engage in a process by which they can solve problems that tend to cross national boundaries – ones that are global in scope.

FOREWARD

This is why the thesis written in the 1980s by this writer did not propose international laws that made Global Armageddon illegal (presumably such a thing is already illegal anyway). The thesis focused more on a framework for decision-making that made the destruction of Earth less likely to occur.

In some respects creating a legal framework to solve problems that come up in the international arena is similar to the method scientists use to discover possible solutions to problems. To oversimplify, a scientist observes a phenomenon, creates a hypothesis to explain it, and then tests the hypothesis through experimentation. Science itself does not explain why the phenomenon exists or how to make it go away if it is a problem that needs solving. The best that science can do is propose and test a theory through a logical process on how to solve a problem, and then show through experimentation how the theory holds up to critical scrutiny. Science offers a method of discovering what the answer to a problem might be. Science does not give an answer once and for all to a given problem.

Quite a few years passed since that thesis was written. Then along came an announcement of something called the New Shape Prize that promised to pay a whole bunch of money to anyone who could, in effect, present a regime that would cause the nations of the world to relent from the path of destruction that they mutually have been following.

FOREWARD

Growing weary of his day job as a lawyer, your humble narrator dusted off his old thesis from his idealistic law school days and gave a bit of a facelift to some of those old ideas and thoughts about what could be done to make nuclear annihilation of the species and the resulting environmental catastrophe a wee bit less likely to come to fruition. Those thoughts and ideas were packaged up in a clever way of literary non-fiction that he hoped the average person would be more interested in reading than, say, a dry academic exercise filled with lots of jargon typically found in treatises on international law and "foreign" policy.

That clever device of literary non-fiction is what you are about to (hopefully) read with eager anticipation and overwhelming delight.

It is called *How to Save the World (in 12 Easy Steps)*.

I hope you enjoy reading it.

PS - I never liked the term "foreign" policy. What the heck is that supposed to mean anyway?

If we are all Citizens of One Earth, how can we be foreigners to one another?

ABOUT THE NEW SHAPE PRIZE

In November 2016, the Global Challenges Foundation issued a call to people around the world to submit their ideas on proposals to provide an improved framework of global governance that would help reduce global catastrophic risks. By the September 2017 deadline, the Foundation had received 2,702 entries from 122 countries.

How to Save the World (In 12 Easy Steps) was one of them.

The call to action by the Foundation said that humankind lives in a global community that is impacted by behavior and decisions of nation-states that have transnational import, the problem of Global Warming and Climate Change being chief among them.

There are other problems, such as other forms of large-scale environmental damage, politically-motivated violence, extreme poverty and rapid population growth. The folks at the Foundation thought that these challenges would be more effectively managed through a collectively binding, long-term decision-making process that takes into account all those concerned – including future generations. So they created something they called the New Shape Prize.

ABOUT THE NEW SHAPE PRIZE

The prize challenged participants to submit alternatives to the present international regime by reforming the current UN system or by proposing completely new forms of global governance. Rules for the Prize stipulated the format of how participants were to make their proposed alternatives, which were to appear under three basic headings:

I. ABSTRACT (No more than 1,000 words). The abstract summarizes the proposed plan being offered by the participant as an alternative to the current world order. The plan is supposed to include (1) the institutions and decision-making processes that were to be implemented, and (2) the means by which decision-makers were to be appointed.

II. DESCRIPTION (No more than 5,500 words). This part of the proposal defines the functional components of the plan, the areas of responsibility and decision-making of each component, and how the overall plan manages current and emerging challenges and risks.

III. ARGUMENTATION (No more than 2,750 words). In this section the proposal advocates a position as to whether the proposed plan meets "assessment criteria" set by the Foundation that were as follows:

ABOUT THE NEW SHAPE PRIZE

(a) **Values**: Decisions must be guided by the good of all humankind and by respect for the equal value of all human beings;

(b) **Capacity**: Critical decisions must be made without crippling delays;

(c) **Effectiveness**: Decisions must be able to handle the global challenges and include means to ensure their implementation;

(d) **Resources and Financing**: The governing body must have the resources to do its job, financed in an equitable manner;

(e) **Trust**: Trust in the governing body must be earned by transparency and insight into its power structures and decision-making;

(f) **Flexibility**: The governing body must allow for revisions and improvements to the way it operates;

(g) **No Abuse of Power**: There must be a system of checks and balances to prevent the governing body from straying from its mandate, or by interfering with the right of self-determination of peoples or nations, or showing favoritism to special interests; and

(h) **Accountability**: The governing body must be held accountable for its actions.

How to Save the World (in 12 Easy Steps) made a pitch, in literary fashion, to answer the call made by the folks over at the Global Challenges Foundation to come up with ideas on

ABOUT THE NEW SHAPE PRIZE

how we can better solve global problems. It was one of over 2,700 entries submitted as part of the New Shape Prize contest. It was not a finalist for the New Shape Prize.

Not even an honorable mention was made of it.

Until now.

TABLE OF CONTENTS

"In order to achieve completeness in our knowledge of nature, we must start from two extremes, from experience and from the intellect itself. ... The former method must conclude with natural laws, which it has abstracted from experience, while the latter must begin with principles, and gradually, as it develops more and more, it becomes ever more detailed."

- Hans Christian Oersted, Danish physicist and chemist (1799)

"Lastly, we have three that raise the former discoveries by experiments into greater observations, axioms, and aphorisms. These we call interpreters of nature."

- Sir Francis Bacon, English philosopher and statesman (1627)

"To explain all nature is too difficult a task for any one man or even for any one age. 'Tis much better to do a little with certainty, and leave the rest for others that come after you, than to explain all things."

- Sir Isaac Newton, English astronomer and physicist (1704)

I. THE TWELVE STEP PROGRAM

Faced with ever increasing demands upon the resources of the Planet Earth, her inhabitants, heretofore seemingly intent on her destruction, suddenly came to the realization that her survival and prosperity was in fact inextricably interwoven with their own, and so a challenge was issued calling for ideas on How to Save the World from the humans who lived there and, in essence, how the species could spare itself from its path of self-destruction.

When the mind and body is bent on self-destruction, the tried and true method of reversing this process involves Twelve Steps. In this case here are those steps:

1. Declare World Citizenship.

All human beings are part of a global community. They share a commons that encompasses all of the Planet Earth. They are all Citizens of that World.

2. Recognize Human Aspirations.

All Citizens of the World are endowed with universally recognized inalienable aspirations that impel them by their nature to improve the human condition for themselves, their kindred, and their fellow World Citizens.

3. Grant Freedom to All World Citizens.

All World Citizens have the freedom to self-determine their destiny and to exercise their free will as to their actions and environment, so long as doing so does not interfere in the ability of others to do likewise.

4. Give Voice to World Citizens.

Allow for the voices of World Citizens to be heard through their appointed representatives who serve as Delegates at the First World Congress.

5. Draft Founding Documents and Select a Situs.

Create the Charter and other Governing Documents for the First World Congress. Select a place where the Congress can convene.

6. Assemble the Founders.

Choose 70 people who subscribe to the Founding Principles to form a council and establish the Laws of Governance for the Council of Founders.

7. Conduct a Census.

Define the populace and the constituencies among the World's Citizens and establish laws and procedures for conducting the First World Census. Use this data to group the World's Citizens within collectives that will ultimately be assigned to delegations to the First World Congress.

8. Convene the First World Congress.

Determine the make-up of the 700 delegations to the First World Congress that shall serve as a forum where the collective voices of World Citizens can be heard. Draw from the Founding Documents to clarify the Mandate of the Congress and set its Rules of Governance.

9. Create Geo-Spheres.

Determine the interlocking system of separate but conjoined geological spheres of the Earth and define how those spheres interact as part of Global Environmental Systems.

10. Establish a Council for Each Geo-Sphere.

Establish mandates for the wise stewardship of Global Environmental Systems by each Geo-Sphere Council, rules for determining the make-up of each Council, and how they are to be governed.

11. Assess the Members.

Assess each delegate to the World Congress and each member of the Geo-Sphere Councils proportionately based on the population they represent to fund the operations of the Congress and the Geo-Spheres.

12. Empower Judicial Review.

Establish Judicial Tribunals in each Geo-Sphere granting to them jurisdiction over questions and claims asserted by any person as a World Citizen, including petitions for the issuance of Writs of Habeas Corpus.

II. THE OLD MAN & THE SEA

A wise man sat upon his usual perch up on a mountainside on the island where he lived, looking out upon the vast ocean that spread out before him as far as his tired old eyes could see. The other inhabitants with whom he shared the island called him the Ancient One.

They all revered the great body of water that surrounded them in a protective embrace, provided the bounty that sustained life, and had so defined the natural world in no uncertain terms and their proper place in it.

Yet they were aware of subtle changes that had been taking place in her magnificence over the years. Her anger seemed more insistent that something was amiss when the winds and rains came with more ferocity during the storms she had always sent near or past them.

King Tides seemed all the more menacing as they crept ever so higher and higher.

The gentle rains came like torrents – or not at all – a feast and famine of life-sustaining water that violently gave, and then did not give, in a pattern that was at first so unfamiliar to them yet was now becoming an unpleasant fact of life that they were forced to accept.

Neither the tired old eyes of the Ancient One nor any of the others could see what lay beyond the distant horizon, but they were aware that in those far-off lands other inhabitants with whom they shared the world had altered the natural order of things in ways that had, quite literally, begun to wash up upon the shores of the place they called home.

No man is an island the Ancient One thought to himself, but what can one man do alone in the face of a global challenge of this magnitude?

The answer, he knew, was nothing.

But he had friends that could help him.

He resolved within himself to call upon the best and the brightest minds he could bring to bear upon the problem. They would come from all walks of life and from each corner of the globe. They would each offer differing perspectives from different disciplines in economics, science, biology, law, philosophy, the arts, and the entire spectrum of thoughtful contemplation from which human civilization had been constructed and would now need to evolve in order to survive.

The Ancient One realized that he would need a frame of reference from which to proceed before recruiting the architects that would create the framework upon which the machinery these new features of human civilization would use to evolve into its next iteration.

He pulled out the treatise he had come across entitled *How to Save the World*, suppressing a chuckle as he scanned over the call for the human species to engage in a Twelve Step Process to overcome its self-destructive tendencies. "This will do as a starting point, I suppose," he said aloud. There was no one else there who heard him.

"I will use this as a framework for a framework that I will show my friends so we can build a framework!"

He set to work.

FOUNDATIONAL PRINCIPLES

The first step in what turned out to be a Three-Part Process was to establish fundamental principles that would lay the groundwork for building consensus among those that inhabit Planet Earth on how best to become wise stewards of her Environmental Systems, both globally and in the immediate environs where they had made their homes.

These Foundational Principles had to consist of universal truths that were universally recognized and accepted universally by all peoples of good faith who ascribe to the notion that all people of the world share the same world within which to carry on their lives and a common destiny as to the shape that world is to take now and into the future.

Here is what the Ancient One came up with:

I. World Citizenship

The First Foundational Principle is existential in nature. Human beings existing on Planet Earth live there as part of one species, one *life form* that takes part in a global system of life forms that interact in a shared environment that knows no artificial boundaries created by the prevailing societal constructs that seek to separate them.

This is not the way things should be but is the nature of things. Declaring that all people of the world are citizens of that world is not to do something new but to simply recognize what already is. The people of the world are the people of the world. They may be induced to believe they are constituents of a geographically-defined subset of that world, either by nation, state, province, city, town, hamlet, neighborhood, home or room within a home, but they are and will always remain part of something larger:

The Human Race.

II. Universal Human Aspirations

The Second Foundational Principle is aspirational in nature. By their nature human beings, although part of the animal kingdom, aspire for more than an existence that consists of a banal cycle of birth, survival, procreation, and then death that seems to define other species with whom they share Planet Earth.

They look for meaning in their lives. They look to the stars and, while they cannot reach them with outstretched arms, they can with their minds and their spirit.

They grapple with the words to define these natural instincts towards improving the human condition for themselves, their loved ones and others who share their world. They are described as springing from "Natural" or "Organic" Law and are usually referred to as "rights." Efforts have been made to identify and to list them by documents such as the *Magna Carta*, the American *Bill of Rights*, and in the *Universal Declaration of Human Rights*.

These efforts are not meant to delimit the full extent of what these aspirations are but to articulate the basic contours of the essence of them and to recognize that the unfettered pursuit of these aspirations (usually referred to as the free exercise of inalienable birthrights) are in tension with organized governments and with one set of people who may not share in the manner by which they are expressed by another.

The natural human inclination to freely think, speak, believe and aspire to greater things should be encouraged and not suppressed either by a government nor by a group or groups of people who have contrary or conflicting thoughts, words, beliefs or aspirations.

III. Self Determination

The Third Principle allows World Citizens to exercise free will. While one aspect of human nature is to have aspirations, another is to act upon them. Citizens of the World yearn to be free to do as they wish.

They should be granted that freedom, so long as what they choose to do does not adversely impact the freedom of others to do likewise.

This includes actions that impact a shared environment. One person acting alone can improve the human condition for that lone person and those in his or her immediate vicinity. Many people acting together can improve their collective lot in life many times over.

They are collectively engaging in self-determination for each individual (if there is a consensus to act as one) and can expand the reach of their benevolent behavior beyond their immediate space, creating or maintaining a shared, beneficial "sphere of influence."

But as that sphere of influence grows larger and larger, the ability of any one individual to truly exercise self-determination diminishes, and the risk that the actions of the many within that sphere will adversely impact those that live within its confines grows.

The ability to exercise self-determination for an individual within a group declines as the group becomes larger and less likely to act by way of consensus.

So, too, does the risk that the actions of the group become detrimental to its constituents and the environment they share.

IV. The Voice of the People

The Fourth Foundational Principle gives World Citizens a voice. For thousands of years the institutions of human civilization have never provided a forum where the voices of all of the citizens of the world can be heard.

Crude measures have been devised where the people of the world can influence the selection of the rulers of their immediate environs and even large swaths of territory expanding out for thousands of miles in all directions. But even the largest of these places (called "nations") do not claim to speak on behalf of everyone.

Even democracies or other forms of government that have elections only purport to hire a sampling of a representative sample of people within its geographic borders that then make decisions as they see fit, regardless of the true will of the people they represent.

Occasionally a plebiscite will express the will of the governed. But it is up to the elites who govern over the people to decide what the government actually does. These elites then send representatives to the United Nations.

The United Nations, although a contradiction in terms, is just that: a league of nations where there is no hint of direct representation of the citizens of the world.

The league is comprised of representatives of the elites who rule over nations.

It acts as a forum for nations, not people.

Now, for the first time in human history, a forum will be created where the voices of the citizens of the world will directly be heard.

That forum is the First World Congress.

ORGANIZATIONAL FOUNDATIONS

The Ancient One was satisfied with the first part of the framework he was building for the Framework that he would ask his friends to help him create.

He had established the Founding Principles for how to go about saving the world that should be universally accepted by the people inhabiting Planet Earth:

(I) that everyone is a Citizen of the World,
(II) that these world citizens have aspirations that are to be respected as a birthright,
(III) that world citizens have the freedom to do as they wish so long as it does not deprive others to do likewise, and

(IV) that the citizens of the world shall have a forum so their voices can be heard.

His next task was to create the second part of the framework for the Framework.

He saw that this part required him to provide the broad outlines of the Organizational Foundations upon which the First World Congress would be based.

Here is what he decided that should look like:

V. Foundational Documents & Situs

Every good First World Congress needs a good Charter. It also needs a place to call home. In order to do this, the Ancient One selected a small group of his fellow wise men and women to help.

He would call this inner circle the Architects. He would recruit the Architects by showing them the framework (which had now become part of the treatise on *How to Save the World*) for the Framework they were to create together.

If they agreed with the framework and its principles, they would join the inner circle that would be the Architects of the First World Congress.

There were seven Architects, representing each of the seven continents of the world.

The Ancient One took Antarctica because he didn't know any wise people that lived there. The others came from the other six continents. Together they assigned tasks to each

Architect over designing and drafting the Charter and other governing documents that would be needed to form the institutions outlined in the framework.

They needed a place to meet.

Their first meeting was on the island where the Ancient One lived. At that meeting, they decided where they could establish the main headquarters of the First World Congress. They also decided on where (and from whom) they could find the resources to fund the nascent organization, its situs, and to pay for the lawyers, scientists, planners and other professionals with whom they needed to consult to draft the Charter and other governing documents and to establish a home base from which they could operate.

VI. The Council of Founders

The first section of the Charter has a section that lays out the Four Founding Principles of World Citizenship.

The next section describes the formation of the Council of Founders.

This is a group of 70 people hand-picked by the Architects to fulfill the mission of the Charter in creating the First World Congress, establishing how delegates to the Congress are to be appointed, and its governing laws.

Each Member of the Council of Founders, by virtue of their appointment as a Member, becomes a Delegate to the 700-Member First Congress. Each Delegate speaks for a constituency of the World's Citizenry.

The 70 Members of the Council each represent their proportionate share of all of the constituencies of the world.

The job of the 70 Members is to jointly define the constituency each represents, and all of the groups within their constituency that make up the 10 Delegates each are assigned. They also create the internal rules by which the Council is to be governed.

VII. The First World Census

Another section of the Charter establishes how the Founders are to define the constituencies that are assigned to Delegates to the Congress through the First World Census. The census gathers information about the peoples of the world and groups them demographically in accordance with the characteristics that can fairly be said to give them an affinity for one another as a group.

Each group, or Collective, of peoples may be defined in the census as sharing common traits such as ethnicity, nationality, culture, religion, and language, but may not be defined by any one, or predominantly by any one, of such traits. The goal of the census is to identify peoples with a common bond with one another who are most likely to speak through a delegate with one voice, not to divide the people of the world along competing racial, ethnic, religious or other grounds that are divisive and unhealthy to harmonious human interaction.

VIII. The First World Congress

The Charter also has a section on the formation of the First World Congress, convened as a forum for the voices of the people of the world to be heard.

Delegates to the Congress make application to the Council of Founders through their designated Council Member to represent a specific Collective or Collectives determined by the Council to be a valid constituency in accordance with its rules.

A Delegate (or Delegation) must provide proof through a plebiscite, signed petition(s) or other means acceptable by the Council, as to the number of World Citizens being represented by that Delegate (and thus the number of votes that may be cast on questions arising before the Congress) the fact that the Delegate/Delegation has been empowered by its purported constituencies to speak for them and demonstrate there are procedures in place to assess the sense of the constituencies regarding specific questions of grave concern that come before the Congress.

Delegates to the First World Congress are convened at such times and pursuant to such rules as are, first, as set forth in the Charter; second, by applicable governing laws as established by the Council of Founders; and lastly, by rules adopted by the Congress itself.

The Congress has no geographically-defined jurisdictional boundaries but asserts no sovereignty over territory subject to the rule of law of sovereign nations.

The Congress does have sovereignty over the situs where the Congress conducts its business and such lands or territories where jurisdiction is ceded to it.

The mandate of the Congress is to provide a forum where the Citizens of the World may have their voices heard concerning matters of concern to them as inhabitants of the Planet Earth so as to build a consensus on how they may best become wise stewards of her Environmental Systems, both globally and in the immediate environs where they have made their homes and live out their lives.

FUNCTIONAL FOUNDATIONS

Turning his attention back to the life-sustaining sea that surrounds him, the Ancient One contemplated the seemingly utopian idea that he and all of the other peoples inhabiting other places in faraway worlds beyond the distant horizon – those he could not see, but somehow could *feel* – were really all citizens of one world, bound together by nature and the laws of human nature.

Could these laws be rendered into concrete form that the ancients had so struggled to articulate in centuries past?

Could the voices of the Citizens of the World be heard through a forum such as the First World Congress? Would anyone listen?

The first parts of the Charter and its other governing documents lay out the principles that will guide the newly-formed forum to achieve its goal of giving voice to the Citizens of the World in their quest to save the world from the self-destructive habits of its inhabitants.

The rest of the Framework breathes life into those voices.

IX. The Geo-Spheres

Consulting with the best and brightest scientists and other wise women and men of the world, the Architects devised a method by which the global environment could be logically segmented into geological spheres that could be fairly described as ecologically distinctive, yet with the knowledge that those spheres all interact with one another as part of one set of Global Environmental Systems.

The guidelines on how these Geo-Spheres are to be defined and where they are located can be found in the Charter. The Council of Founders is charged in the Charter with establishing the actual contours of the Geo-Spheres, based on the best available science and the guidelines for giving them shape as provided in the Charter.

The Charter makes clear that, while the Geo-Spheres attempt to break Global Environmental Systems down into manageable areas of Planet Earth, there are no real boundaries between them, their imaginary boundaries shift over time, they at times overlap, and are always just parts of one set of dynamic Global Environmental Systems.

X. Geo-Sphere Councils

A council is formed for each Geo-Sphere. As stated in the Charter, the mandate for each council is to provide a forum whereby the inhabitants within the Geo-Sphere have a say in the wise stewardship of the land, sea and air within their sphere consistent with the natural environmental forces at work within that sphere, as well as the processes taking place in the wider global environment.

The councils take into account the impact of human activities and human alterations to the natural environment, provide information and analysis as to what the inhabitants can expect concerning changes taking place in the environment within the Geo-Sphere, make recommendations for actions to be taken to mitigate or reverse adverse consequences of human activities and development on the environment, and undertake direct action where its resources and capabilities allow.

A Delegate of the World Congress is assigned to each Geo-Council to serve as Chairperson by the Council of

Founders, commissioned to carry out the mandate as provided in the Charter.

By law, the Founders establish the perquisites for an individual, group, government, entity, or other person to be admitted as a Geo-Council Member, which shall include an acceptance of the mandate of the Council and the mission of the Congress, an agreement to abide by the Charter, Laws and Rules of the Council and Congress and demonstrate that the member is empowered to speak for a substantial number of constituent World Citizens that regularly inhabit the Geo-Sphere.

Within the Charter and governing laws of the Council of Founders are the rules for selecting applicants to be appointed as members of the Geo-Sphere Councils, grounds for expulsion, grounds for an appeal to the Congress for any decision or action taken by the Geo-Sphere Council, and the governing laws applicable to the conduct of the affairs of each.

The Chairperson of each is the facilitator of the work to be conducted by the Geo-Sphere Council and, together with the Council itself, sets the internal rules by which it governs its affairs.

XI. Assessments Per Capita

Operations of the Congress and the Geo-Spheres are funded by assessments.

The costs of operations are determined annually and set forth in a detailed budget presented by the Council of Founders, which shall be deemed approved unless, pursuant to rules established in the Charter, one or more line items are eliminated or reduced by vote of the Congress.

Each Delegate is assessed a share of the costs to operate the Congress (as determined by the approved budget) in proportion to the population that Delegate represents as compared to the whole.

The members of each Geo-Sphere Council are assessed in like fashion to fund the operations of the Geo-Sphere. Membership in the Council is conditioned on payment of the assessment. The budget and assessments shall be determined by each Council and submitted by the Chairperson to the Council of Founders for approval as provided by the procedures set forth in the Charter and Laws of the Founders.

XII. Judicial Review

As a condition to participating in a Geo-Sphere, all members consent to the jurisdiction of any judicial tribunal established for the Council by the Congress to adjudicate matters of concern arising from within that Geo-Sphere.

The Charter limits the reach of the matters that may be adjudicated in such tribunals to those provided for by the principles and mission of the Congress.

Any World Citizen who can demonstrate a bona fide domicile within the Geo-Sphere has standing to invoke the jurisdiction of the tribunal to adjudicate any claims that an action of a member of the Geo-Sphere adversely impacts that Citizen in the lawful exercise of his or her entitlements under the Charter and Laws of the Congress and may request relief from the tribunal. That relief includes declaratory relief or the issuance of a writ of *habeas corpus*.

Tribunals of a Geo-Sphere are established by the Congress and funded by the Geo-Sphere Council but operate independently of them.

Judicial officers are nominated by the Council of Founders, subject to confirmation by vote of the Geo-Sphere Council. The rules for nomination, confirmation and removal from office are as determined by the Charter and Governing Laws of the Council of Founders.

Decisions of a tribunal may be appealed to supervisory tribunals or courts established by the Congress or to existing institutions, such as the International Court of Justice, the European Court of Human Rights, and the Inter-American Court of Human Rights.

III. THE INQUISITION

Gathered in the main conference room, the group of Inquisitors met yet again to further vet the remaining submissions out of the 2,702 they had received that offered solutions to the global challenge that faced humankind: how to avert an almost certain, looming environmental catastrophe that could usher in the extinction of the species caused, ironically enough, by its own suicidal tendencies.

Some stared, weary-eyed, at the stack of remaining submissions, their initial enthusiasm for the project buried somewhere behind heavy eyelids stewed in stupefied, sleep-deprived brains assailed by a flood of words and pages filled with ideas and frameworks and citations and stratagems and models and arguments and on and on into the night.

One of their number rescued a submission from the slush pile if for no other reason than it came as a welcome relief to the mind-numbing repetition of papers that followed the submission guidelines in true lawyerly fashion, replete with language only a judge of lawyers submitting briefs could love. Little did the Inquisitor know that the author of *How to Save the World (In Twelve Easy Steps)* was in fact a lawyer himself who had written many briefs, more than a few of which inspired published opinions written by judges who took a fancy to the things he had to say, more often than not agreeing with them.

But, alas, the brief-writing days of the lawyer had long since passed. He was, after all, a writer trapped in a lawyer's body. So *How to Save the World* took on a certain literary flair. Maybe it would not garner a Nobel Peace Prize for the Global Challenges Foundation, but at least it served as an easy read during those long-suffering nights of reading through page after page of ways to reform the moribund U.N. Even better, it fell well short of the word count limits.

This treatise did not read as if it even tried to adhere to the mechanical, rigid rules of engagement applicable to the other submissions. But on closer examination, perhaps such is not quite the case. Sure, the work for all appearances looked as though it was something the ordinary person of even modest intellectual curiosity might actually buy at a bookstore (or from Amazon) and even make it halfway through without falling asleep.

But hidden in the cute analogy to the Twelve Step Process by which the afflicted overcome their addictions is some semblance of an "Abstract."

The fanciful tale of the Ancient One and his group of Architects cleverly disguises what is, in fact, a "Description of the Model" for the First World Congress.

But what of the argumentative rationale section of the piece?

Picking through the subliminal messages contained in the story of the Ancient One's framework within a framework to guide him and his friends in building "The Framework," the Inquisitors could divine the makings of something that might just pass muster when it comes to meeting the criteria for the New Shape contest.

Core Values. Talk about core values! The Ancient One spends so much time going on and on about the fundamental rights of all peoples of the world, you expect him to levitate at any moment.

But he was right to do that.

At the core of enduring constitutional systems is the idea that there are fundamental values expressed in documents such as the Bill of Rights to the United States Constitution (as well as the Universal Declaration of Human Rights) conferring upon all people legal protection to aspire to living a life consistent with those values.

Capacity to Govern versus Abuse of Power. Of concern to the Inquisitors is the capacity of any global institution (such as the U.N.) to make decisions and to take action without crippling delays or obstructions caused by those in a position to sabotage the process so as to meet their own needs as opposed to those of the world. At the same time there is a recognized need to create a regime that prevents an abuse of the exercise of power by the players who participate in the governance of such a proposed global institution.

An accommodation must be struck between these two extremes.

In the case of the First World Congress, the Ancient One and his fellow Architects, obviously having received a number of briefs from some American lawyers, incorporate a system of checks and balances into their Framework.

The Congress, comprised as a large body of 700 Delegates, has the potential to become a lumbering blob of people who are not able, due to sheer numbers, to do much of anything. But the Congress is designed as a deliberative body and is supposed to deliberate on things, not do things.

The potential for the abuse of power by this sleepy giant are extremely low. The impetus for action resides in a sub-group of the Congress (the Founders), regional Geo-Spheres, and the judicial tribunals.

Except for provisions within the Charter that limit them, the Founders have the ability to create their own laws of governance and have few impediments to taking action but at the same time have checks on their decision-making in various respects by the Congress, the Geo-Spheres and the tribunals. Similarly, the Geo-Spheres are granted decision-making power within their sphere of influence, limited by the parameters set by the Charter and the Founders.

The judicial tribunals operate independent of the other World Congress bodies, with a check on their power being the ability of the Founders to appoint (with consent by the Geo-Sphere) judicial officers, or remove them, and the right of appeal to a higher court of decisions made by a tribunal judge who may have made a poor decision.

Effectiveness. "But this will never work," one of the Inquisitors blurts out. "How is a blob of humanity 700 strong supposed to do the things that need to be done, even if they have these crazy 'Geo-Orbs' floating around helping them? This is too heavy of a lift."

This is to beg the question of the Global Challenge itself. Design a world government that will brush aside nation states and handle climate change, species extinction, famine, droughts, tsunamis, violent storms, rising sea levels, disease, pestilence, swarms of locusts and whatever else Mother Nature has planned for us? Or somehow reform the hapless U.N. to take this on?

Will a system of Geo-Spheres reporting to a World Congress and subject to judicial review be able to handle these problems? The real answer is that, by themselves, they are not intended to do that.

They are but a vehicle for stakeholders and players to engage in joint decision-making on behalf of the people who live in their region of the world to preserve, protect and sustain the environment in which they live.

The stakeholders have every incentive to be effective in meeting these challenges within their sphere of influence and seeing to it that the other players in other spheres do likewise. After all, radioactive fallout, to take an extreme example, is not healthy for the people who live there when a nuclear bomb is dropped in your neighborhood.

Then the wind blows, and it ends up in your next-door neighbor's yard . . .

Resources & Financing. Raising funds by assessments of Delegates in proportion to the population they represent is the most equitable means to finance the operations of the Congress. Since the decisions of the body are made per capita, payment for operating the body should be as well.

If the body is unable to justify the costs of its decision-making to the people on whose behalf those decisions are made, they will have a more difficult time persuading their constituents to pay those costs.

The Delegates and the body as a whole therefore have every incentive for effective decision-making.

Similarly, the stakeholders and players who comprise the Geo-Spheres (some of which will be nation-states) will gladly fund the costs of operating them so long as they are effective in their mission. The more that is expected of them collectively by their constituents, the more funding they will receive, so long as they meet those expectations.

Trust & Insight. "What sort of credibility does a plan that is based on the ideas of a fictional character called the 'Ancient One' and his cadre of buddies who call themselves the 'Architects' have?" another world-weary Inquisitor asks to no one in particular. "Reads like a scene from one of the Matrix movies with the Oracle and the Architect."

HOW TO SAVE THE WORLD

To be sure, any proposal to form a new global institution that has any hope of achieving the lofty goals set by the Inquisitors needs credible authorship that no single person (or group) submitting a paper to them has any chance of providing. Even Yoda couldn't do it.

The Inquisitors would do well to take heed of what the Ancient One proposes.

His is not a proposal on How to Save the World. His is but a framework for the best and the brightest to use to build the Framework upon which the principles, institutions and mechanisms can be mounted to give the people of the world a chance to save themselves.

In essence, that Framework proposes the creation of a forum for ideas on how to save the world, as opposed to a sovereign entity that imposes ideas it comes up with on the inhabitants of her. The fora proposed by the Ancient One do not provide the answers to the question "How to Save the World" but the means by which those answers can be found by the best and the brightest people of the World.

To have any credibility those who are chosen to have a voice in the institutions created by the Architects have to speak plainly, openly and intelligently with words and actions that gain currency among the people of the world because those words and actions make sense, prove to be accurate and are consistent with the mission that caused the Global Challenge to be issued in the first place.

The power of the institutions proposed by the Ancient One is, in essence, the power of persuasion. Without an honest and open discussion, they have none.

Flexibility. Drawing some welcome laughter, another Inquisitor asks, "Other than probably being a yogi, what flexibility does this Yoda character offer in his ideas about how to save the world?"

Sitting in a lotus position, the Ancient One (no doubt addressing this impish Inquisitor as "Grasshopper") would gently remind the Inquisitors that to be strong enough to endure, a framework must be rigid and firm, despite having spaces between its girders that you can see through.

Otherwise, it is not a framework.

It is just a house of cards.

Essential to the task at hand is to provide the basic, universal principles that define the laws of nature and of human nature. These principles are set in concrete.

Their essential nature has not changed over the ages and will never change. The only thing that changes are the words we use in an effort to describe them.

These principles are like guideposts used as pillars that make the Framework stand erect, holding forth against the elements that might otherwise erode them.

Including time.

A good framework, such as the one proposed by the Ancient One and the Architects, attaches platforms to these pillars that are to hold the institutions it creates in place, anchored to the pillars of principles. A sturdier foundation for a World Stage could not be conceived.

How the players on that stage perform is where the flexibility the Inquisitors seek can be found.

They write their own scripts. They make their own rules that provide their choreography.

They perform and the audience either applauds or sends them back to re-write their scripts, re-design their choreography, rehearse more, or get better actors.

"Is not all the world a stage, Grasshopper?" asks the Ancient One rhetorically.

Protecting Sovereignty/Preserving Equality. Their fears that the First World Congress would run amok having been allayed by the sophisticated system of checks and balances baked into the Framework, some among the Inquisitors still wondered how the Ancient One would respond (if he were a real person) to concerns about the potential of the First World Congress to interfere in the internal affairs of sovereign states, or favor special interests, either those of a sovereign nation or other world actors.

"I see, swarms of Grasshoppers," he would reply, "that on the one hand, you wish for the world's savior to be effective in saving humans from themselves, but on the other, to be careful that it does not interfere with what they are doing." He would then, no doubt, answer this riddle by posing to the Inquisitors the Zen koan question that asks:

What is the sound of one hand clapping?

As conceived by the Architects, the Framework they propose does not attempt to exert sovereignty over people or nations. The only power it has is the power of persuasion.

All Citizens of the World are given a voice, indirectly through their representatives in the Geo-Spheres and more directly in the Congress itself, to persuade others that their view of what should be done is the correct one.

Should their ideas not gain purchase, they will float aimlessly in a sea of other similar ideas headed nowhere, eventually disappearing into the abyss.

The Framework provides a means for all voices to be heard. The only favoritism is towards those that express ideas that float to the top of the cacophony of those judged less worthy by the blob of humanity charged with the task of listening to all who wish to be heard.

Accountability. By this time all tension had left the bodies of the assembled Inquisitors.

Some sat in the lotus position and were consciously breathing. Others were meditating. Some searched Google about what the sound of one hand clapping means.

One fell asleep.

They did not have to concern themselves about the ideas of the fictional old wise man on the top of a non-existent island mountain and whether his idea of creating the First World Congress, Geo-Spheres and such would suffice to hold the decision-makers within that model of governance accountable to the Citizens of the World for their actions.

How is one held accountable for expressing an opinion about what should be done when that idea proves to be not very good in practice? How does one call another to account for expressing a thought that is not well thought out, or an idea that sounds crazy?

A place that serves as a clearinghouse for information and ideas is held accountable by the readers and listeners who consume them and judge their quality by either accepting or rejecting them.

That place in and of itself does not take action for which it must be held to account, regardless of whether the idea that led to that action was spawned by the exchange of ideas hosted by a forum such as this.

If an action promoted by the Congress proves beneficial, its credibility is enhanced and its power when recommending other actions will increase.

If the Congress promotes a bad idea that yields bad results, it is held accountable by its diminished capacity to recommend other actions in the future.

The Ancient One offers a means by which those Homo sapiens that wish to save their world from destruction and their species from extinction can have their voices heard.

He leaves accountability for their actions squarely where it rightly belongs:

Their shoulders.

John Singer Sargent, *Atlas and the Hesperides*, circa 1922-1925,
oil on canvas, Museum of Fine Arts, Boston (public domain).

HOW TO SAVE THE WORLD

SRB McKenzie, *Ancient One as Atlas* (cover art), 2023,
Englewood, Florida (with permission)

www.12easysteps.info

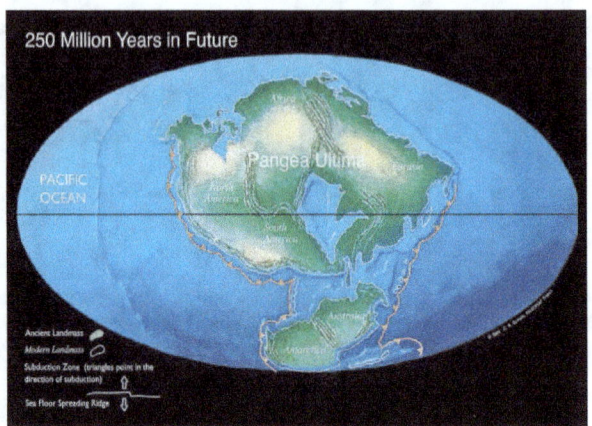

Scotese, C.R., 2001, *Pangea Ultima*, Atlas of Earth History,
Volume 1, Paleogeography, PALEOMAP Project,
Arlington, Texas, 57 pp

SRB McKenzie, *Pangea Ultima* (back cover art), 2025,
Englewood, Florida (with permission)

www.12easysteps.info

About the Artwork

Front cover:

Interpretation of the Ancient One shouldering Pangea (as it was previously thought to exist) by artist SRB McKenzie (based on *Atlas and the Hesperides* by John Singer Sargent (1925)(Museum of Fine Arts, Boston).

Back cover:

SRB McKenzie's interpretation of Pangea Proxima (circa 250 million years in the future).

About the Author

Bret Shawn Clark is an attorney, author and amateur poet based in the seaside town of Englewood, Florida, where he has recently survived a series of violent weather events predicted in his Cli-Fi novel, *20/20*.

Also from B Shawn Clark:

Clark, B. *The New Great Replacement Theory: Using Humanitarian Law to Revive Civil Liberties in an Era of Retrenchment* (January, 2025) International Law Quarterly, volume XLI, no.1

Clark, B. *Trading Places: Realignment of Turtle Island at the Subnational Level* Intermestic Diplomacy for States and First Nations in North America (October, 2025) International Law Quarterly, volume XLI, no.3

20/20 (http://www.2020-thebook.com/)